Life Is Like a Box of Chocolates...

AND OTHER MOTHERLY WISDOM FROM THE MOVIES

Other Books by Joe Garner

We Interrupt This Broadcast
And the Crowd Goes Wild
And the Fans Roared
Echoes of Notre Dame Football
Stay Tuned
Now Showing
Made You Laugh

Life Is Like a Box of Chocolates...

AND OTHER MOTHERLY WISDOM FROM THE MOVIES

A Tribute to Mom

JOE GARNER

Andrews McMeel
Publishing

Kansas City

05 06 07 08 09 INL 10 9 8 7 6 5 4 3 2 1

Library of Congress Cataloging-in-Publication Data

Garner, Joe.
    Life is like a box of chocolates—and other motherly wisdom from the movies : a tribute to mom / Joe Garner.
        p. cm.
    ISBN 0-7407-4179-9
        1. Mothers in motion pictures. I. Title.
PN1995.9.M63G37 2005
791.43'635252—dc22

2004062345

Book design by Holly Camerlinck

Attention: Schools and Businesses

Andrews McMeel books are available at quantity discounts with bulk purchase for educational, business, or sales promotional use. For information, please write to: Special Sales Department, Andrews McMeel Publishing, 4520 Main Street, Kansas City, Missouri 64111.

To Mom,
for all that you are . . .
for all that you do.

Contents

Acknowledgments

Once again, thank you to everyone at Andrews McMeel Publishing, especially Chris Schillig and her exceptional staff and designers Tim Lynch and Holly Camerlinck, copy chief Michelle Daniel, and administrative assistant JuJu Johnson. Thank you to Kristine Campbell and Courtney Moilanen and the talented group in the Andrews McMeel public relations department for getting the word out.

Thank you also to my agent, Sloan Harris.

I am especially grateful to Abigail Ray for her talent and dedication to this and every project at GCC.

Once again, thank you to Chris Monte for his creative and masterful editing and to Jim Castle for his imaginative menu and graphic designs for the DVD.

I am grateful to my bookkeeper (and mother of four!) Janel Syverud for making sure that everything flows smoothly at GCC.

Thank you to Suzy Vaughn & Associates and Stephan Michaels for their skillful diplomacy in handling the studio clearances and talent permissions.

I am particularly grateful to all of the wonderful actors for allowing me to include their touching and memorable performances.

Thank you to Larry McCallister at Paramount Pictures, Liz Cooper at Carlton Films, Jeremy Laws and Roni Lubliner at Universal Studios, Steven Shareshian, Paul Brooks, Peter Friedlander, and Eric Paulson at Playtone and Gold Circle Films for providing these motion picture moments.

Thank you to Deidre Thieman at Universal Studios, Stephanie Sue at Paramount Pictures, Geoff Murillo and Jeff Briggs at Warner Bros., Jay Williams at Shooting Star, Howard and Ron Mandelbaum and Robert Milite at Photofest, Jenni Rosenthal at AP Wide World, and Chad Witt at Getty Images for providing the very best photographs.

Thank you to my wife Colleen, who is also a wonderful mother to my son James (J.B.) and my daughter Jillian. And thank you to my parents, especially my mom Betty Garner, for making all of this possible.

> *"Everyone has their own destiny, and you have to do the best with what God gave you," Mrs. Gump carefully explained to her son, Forrest, as he sat devotedly at her bedside.*
>
> *"What's my destiny, Mama?" Forrest asked.*
>
> *"You're going to have to figure that out for yourself," she replied. "Life is like a box of chocolates, Forrest. You never know what you're going to get."*
>
> —A MOTHER'S ADVICE FROM *Forrest Gump*

Motherhood is the noblest of callings, and those who answer the call are at once required to perform an astounding number of roles: protector, nurturer, adviser. And with life's unexpected adversities, mothers are expected to possess an astounding array of qualities: forgiveness, acceptance, trust, sacrifice, and—especially—unconditional love.

Motherhood has been depicted in art and literature throughout time, and thanks to some gifted filmmakers and talented actresses, it has also been celebrated throughout motion picture history. Who can forget the fiercely protective Aurora Greenway (Shirley MacLaine) in *Terms of Endearment*; the unconditional love of Rusty Dennis (Cher) in *Mask*; or the sagacious family matriarch, Maria Portokalos (Lainie Kazan), in *My Big Fat Greek Wedding*?

Life Is Like a Box of Chocolates . . . and Other Motherly Wisdom from the Movies is a celebration of the wonderful qualities of motherhood and its portrayal in film. The accompanying DVD contains the scene from a motion picture that best illustrates one aspect of a mother's love. These magnificent traits are the focus of each chapter, told through real-life stories of how these traits have been put to the test, as well as the stories of what inspired the featured scene.

Moviegoers have watched and cherished many unforgettable performances of motherhood on the silver screen, and have locked them into their hearts and memories: the hardheaded Yankee common sense of Ethel Thayer (Katharine Hepburn) in *On Golden Pond;* the selfless nurturing of Kate Gulden (Meryl Streep) in *One True Thing;* the heartbreaking sacrifice of Khaila Richards (Halle Berry) in *Losing Isaiah;* and the stoic pride of Ying Ying St. Clair (France Nuyen) in *The Joy Luck Club.*

Every one of these stories and timeless scenes in *Life Is Like a Box of Chocolates . . .* will remind mothers of just how precious a gift they are.

I hope your mother enjoys this multimedia tribute.

Life Is Like a Box of Chocolates...

AND OTHER MOTHERLY WISDOM FROM THE MOVIES

Chapter 1

A MOTHER'S

Acceptance

I gave you life so that you could live it.

—Maria Portokalos, *My Big Fat Greek Wedding*

It's every mother's nightmare: Your daughter drags home her new boyfriend, a heavily tattooed thug with a pierced tongue who communicates in primitive grunts and bears a striking resemblance to the No. 1 fugitive on the FBI's Most Wanted list. Just before he whisks your lit- tle princess away on the back of his Harley, she shoots you a dreamy eyed look and mouths silently, "Isn't he great?"

Maybe the idea of stashing her away in a convent for the next thirty or forty years seems like an attractive solution; at the very least, a *serious* discussion about her

judgment is in order. But at what point does a mother cut her losses and decide it's better to accept her kids' choices—however unusual or misguided they may seem—rather than cause herself, and her child, endless heartache by objecting? Finding that delicate balance between mama hen authority and permissive parenting is one of the toughest jobs a mother faces in life.

"The mother-child relationship is paradoxical and, in a sense, tragic," wrote the eminent psychologist Erich Fromm. "It requires the most intense love on the mother's side, yet this very love must help the child grow away from the mother, and to become fully independent." Whether that independence manifests itself in a fifth-grader's desire for blue hair and an earring or the more serious issue of a young adult's "alternative" lifestyle, a mom must be prepared to spring into action— wheedling, cajoling, chastising, and, when necessary, setting aside her own strong opinions in order to validate her child's worth as a person.

"You do not change your kids, you don't—you love them for what they are," says Gloria Mireles, whose teenage son, after years of bullying and painful introspection, confided to her that he was gay. Although Frankie's homosexuality was opposed by Gloria's deep Catholic

faith, she did not hesitate to give him her blessing. "I'll never forget that day," remembered Frankie. "There were tears in her eyes when she said, 'You're my son, I love you.' And she said, 'That—you know, that's all that matters . . . Whoever made fun of you, show them. Show them you can be somebody better.'"

It is natural for parents to want their children to think and act like them; our kids, after all, are in many ways reflections of ourselves. But the greatest gift a mother can give is not her ideas and opinions; it is her love and acceptance. As the poet Kahlil Gibran wrote of children: "You may give them your love but not your

thoughts, for they have their own thoughts . . . Seek not to make them like you." This is especially true as children grow into adolescence and adulthood, since their decisions concerning romance, fashion, sexuality, careers, and personal style sometimes rub us the wrong way and we are forced to confront the divide between our own wishes and their happiness.

When there is a cultural element involved, for example, parents having been raised in a much different environment than their children, family friction can become particularly intense.

No film has tackled those cultural questions of acceptance with more truthfulness and heartwarming humor than My *Big Fat Greek Wedding,* the tale of a first-generation Greek American woman who finds love with a WASPy vegetarian schoolteacher—against the initial objections of her large, loud, and very opinionated family. And no film has better portrayed the uncanny ability of mothers to overcome their own prejudices in order to make their children happy.

"Women all feel this [family] pressure to marry within the fold, within the same flock that we're in," says the film's writer and star, Nia Vardalos, who based the story of Toula Portokalos on her real-life experiences courting and marrying a non-Greek man. "My family was not interested in meeting [my fiancé] because he wasn't Greek," she recalls. "It's not that they had any-thing against him. It's just that my family believes that there are two types of people: Greeks and those who wish they were Greek."

Her purpose in making the film, she says, was "to show the sometimes suffocating but all-encompassing love of a Greek family." That all-encompassing love finds its most intense expression in Toula's mother Maria (Lainie Kazan), whose wisdom and open-mindedness eventually win the day for her beleaguered daughter. This is no mean feat in a family whose home itself has been transformed into a conspicuous architectural testament to Hellenic pride, and whose xenophobic patriarch considers Greek marriage and the bearing of Greek children the *only* proper calling for women.

In the film's most poignant scene, Toula sits in bed the night before her wedding, worrying about the effect her marriage will have on her father, who seems to suffer epileptic fits every time he comes into contact with her fiancé. Maria, who has made her peace with her daughter's decision after first balking at the idea of interethnic nuptials, consoles Toula, assuring her that her happiness is all that matters.

In a gentle whisper, she informs Toula that after all the wars in her country, she came to America hoping for a better life for her children, one free of restrictions and oppression. "We came here for you, so you could live. I gave you life so that you could *live* it." In the glow of

family warmth and acceptance, Toula, Maria, and Toula's grandmother gather around a box of the family's matrimonial keepsakes in preparation for the big day as the scene ends.

"I wanted to show a moment of wisdom that gets passed down to me, so I wrote that speech," says Vardalos.

"And I thought, when we were shooting it, 'If this doesn't show a mother-daughter relationship, then nothing will.'"

In the end, Maria Portokalos comes to represent that special magic that belongs to mothers—the capacity for loving acceptance and tolerance. Mothers must also realize that their children are not empty vessels to be filled with opinions but rather unique individuals whose dreams and decisions in life—although they may not always agree with their parents' wishes—are worthy of support and respect.

Interestingly, the film might never have been made if Vardalos' real-life father had had his way. When the twenty-year-old had decided on a career, she went to speak with her dad. "I said to him, 'Dad, I want to be an actress,'" she recalls. "He ignored me, so I said it again. He said, 'I heard you, a teacher.'" Luckily, mom came to the rescue.

Although she shared some of Vardalos' father's fears, her mother supported her decision because she knew the challenge would make her happy. "My mom raised me to be fearless," Vardalos says. "So I took a chance and then it worked. It worked. If it hadn't worked, at least I took the chance."

A mother is the truest friend we have, when trials heavy and sudden fall upon us; when adversity takes the place of prosperity; when friends who rejoice with us in our sunshine desert us; when trouble thickens around us, still will she cling to us, and endeavor by her kind precepts and counsels to dissipate the clouds of darkness, and cause peace to return to our hearts.

—Washington Irving

Chapter 2

A MOTHER'S

Nurturing Love

*It's so much easier to choose to love the things that you have—and you have
so much—instead of always yearning for what you're missing or what it is
you're imagining you're missing. It's so much more peaceful.*

—KATE GULDEN, *One True Thing*

Children have many teachers throughout their lives, but no one plays a bigger role in nurturing that life than their original teacher, their mother. For the first five years of life, a mother is the focus of her child's entire world—from its total dependency as an infant, through first steps, to that first day of school, a mother is the center of the child's universe.

She nurtures by loving, feeding, clothing, bathing, talking, hugging, playing, and teaching. That interaction prepares the child for the world outside the nursery;

it is the prototype for every societal connection they will encounter in life.

James Kimmel, PhD, writes, "The prolonged mother-child bond is the root of human sociability, and the nurturing response of the mother to her child became a model for human interaction. It prepares both female and male children to live in a world where attachment to, caring about, and collaborating with other humans is natural to life."

Pity the poor child who grows up without that support. Dr. Kimmel says it's a recipe for disaster: "[They] try to satisfy the emptiness inside by attaching to possessions and wealth and by compulsive, self-relating addictions to food, alcohol, drugs, and unloving sex. But these dependencies always fail because they reinforce our feeling of separateness in the world."

Scientists are now discovering that a nurturing mother is important to an infant for more than psychological reasons—there is a physical factor involved. Someone who fosters interaction with an infant helps stimulate the child's brain. In turn, that stimulation forces the brain to form more complex electrical contacts that may actually make the child smarter.

Experiments have suggested that mothers' nurturing "stimulates neural connections in their babies' brains and enhances learning." Registered nurse Mary Ann Rollano writes that you can see the process working when a mother looks at her child. "The mother-child connection is not just emotional, but physical," she says. "Mothers are sensitive to facial expressions, and babies are wired to respond in kind. We are neurologically (as in forever) programmed to be connected to our children."

This is a connection that grows stronger every day, a bond that ties mother and child together for life. In the beginning, of course, a baby literally can't survive without her. There comes a time, however, when every mother must allow her child to fend for itself or risk crippling it. It's so contrary to the nurturing instinct that it is one of the toughest things a mom will ever have to face.

Author and psychotherapist Polly Berrien Berends is no stranger to this phenomenon. In fact, she experienced it with her own child. "What helps them most along their way," she writes, "is seeing how we respond when we stumble or lose our way. One of my sons had trouble learning to ride a bike. I'd run alongside; he'd pedal. But as soon as I'd let go, he'd give up. After days of futile practice . . . I recognized the fear of hurt and failure that I was bringing to the task, my overprotectiveness, and the notion that somehow his life and everything in it depended on me. I realized that he couldn't let go of me until I let go of him. 'Too much mother!' I thought. At once a fresh idea came to me. To my son (and myself) I said, 'Do you really believe that of all of the children on earth, God picked you out to be the one who can't ride a

bike?' Startled recognition flashed in his eyes. I went inside. He went off and rode his bike."

Sometimes, despite the best nurturing, a family becomes disconnected. That's what the movie *One True Thing* is about—the utter importance of reconnecting with the ones you love and the ones who love you, while you still can. It's also about the complicated relationship between a woman who's a traditional nurturing mother and an ambitious daughter who's rejected her mother's values to pursue a career.

The movie was adapted from the best-selling novel by Anna Quindlen. In the film, the mother, Kate Gulden (Meryl Streep) knows that her daughter, Ellen (Renée Zellweger), has never really connected with her but has always been in awe of her literary professor father, George (William Hurt)—even following in her father's footsteps by becoming a writer. Kate desperately wants her daughter to understand the fulfillment of her "ordinary life," the nobility of raising a family, the comfort of being involved in her community, and the pride in keeping a house and a long and imperfect marriage together.

Director Carl Franklin explains, "Ellen has never really valued her mother, and I think this is a common problem between daughters and mothers of this generation. Until she goes back home, Ellen just sees her mother as shallow, but she doesn't realize all the intelligence, wisdom, responsibility, and care that are just under

the surface. And what Kate teaches Ellen is that 'the most important thing is to really be alive in this world and heal yourself and your relationships while you can.'"

Meryl Streep, who loved the novel, and lobbied to play Kate, says she related to what Quindlen was writing about on a personal level. "Anna and I are of the generation of women that was seduced into the pursuit of outward achievements and success on a different scale than . . . things that are unmeasurable, like raising a child well, or doing a good job at home . . . But they raised daughters

who expected to make a mark on the wider world and use their education for something more than running their house."

In the beginning of the movie, Kate, a vital woman, is diagnosed with terminal cancer. As Kate's life ebbs away, George tells their daughter she must move back home to take care of her mother. Ellen resists, knowing it will put her career in jeopardy, but her father prevails with guilt. "You've got a Harvard education, but where is your heart?"

Gradually the women switch roles—as Kate gets weaker, Ellen takes over. Ellen, who initially looked down upon her "housewife" mother, becomes the family's nurturer and finally begins to appreciate what an incredible woman her mother is.

In one of the film's most poignant scenes, Kate is near death, and wants to know, more than anything, that her daughter understands her, and that she has her priorities straight—to cherish the people you love while you still can. The scene is heartbreaking, yet life-affirming. When it is over, you know that Ellen now understands her mother, has reconnected with her, and will be a more complete person because of it.

It's a lesson Meryl Streep, who has four children of her own, learned from her own mother. "My mother was and is my role model," she says. "Not precisely for what she did in her life, but for the way she's always done everything. She always started the day singing, she loves a good joke, she has energy and verve, wit and great natural graciousness . . . I think the best role models for women and girls are people who are fruitfully and confidently themselves, who bring light into the world."

A mother nurtures and brings light into the world for her children. She does this not simply by bearing those children, but rather by polishing, grinding, shaping, and buffing them until they shine bright—bright as the love with which she's filled them.

The mother's heart is the child's schoolroom.

—HENRY WARD BEECHER

Chapter 3

A MOTHER'S

Unconditional Love

You're more beautiful on the inside than most people.

—RUSTY DENNIS, *Mask*

When Rusty Dennis's young son Rocky came to her crying that the other kids at the playground were making fun of him, she told him not to worry. Although Rocky suffered from a genetic disease that resulted in massive deformation of his head and face, Rusty never missed an opportunity to instill in him just how beautiful he was.

"I told him when they laugh at you, *you* laugh at you," she says. "If you act beautiful, you'll be beautiful and they'll see that and love you. You see, I believe the universe will support anything you want to believe."

There is little in this world that rivals the power of a mother's love. From the moment your child comes into the world, you shower them with warmth and affection and offer hope and guidance, even during the tough times. And like Rocky, most of us know that whatever happens, whatever children may say or do, whatever curves life throws in their direction, you will never stop loving them.

Writer and motivational speaker Mike Staver, in a story first published in *Chicken Soup for the Mother's Soul,* remembered the gift his mother gave to him when he was an angry, rebellious adolescent—a treasure he has carried with him his entire life. One night, after a partic-

ularly difficult day, he found an envelope under his pillow. In it was a note from his mother that read:

Mike, I know life is hard right now, I know you are frustrated and I know we don't do everything right. . . . Just know that no matter where you go or what you do in your life . . . I'm here for you and I love you—that will never change.

Love, Mom.

"Today when the sea of life gets stormy," Mike says, "I know that just under my pillow there is that love—consistent, abiding, unconditional love—that changes lives."

Not every choice a child makes in life delights his or her parents. Sometimes a child's decisions meet with skepticism or outright disapproval, especially when those choices conflict with a parent's values or strongly held opinions. But while disappointments and bad feelings may come and go, unconditional love remains forever.

"Unconditional love means that I cannot always predict my reaction or guarantee my strength," author and priest John Powell explains. But it means a commitment to your growth and happiness, that I will always accept you and always love you."

Fear of his mother's reaction to his homosexuality forced thirty-two-year-old "Alan" to keep his secret from her for more than a dozen years. When he finally did sit down with his parents to break the news, he had no idea

what to expect, but he knew he couldn't bear the thought of losing them. "Alan" shared the seminal moment in his life on the Gay & Lesbian Issues Web site, hoping that others would be inspired by his story.

"I am so disappointed in you," his mother declared the instant after he had told them. "I am disappointed that you didn't think that your father and I didn't love you enough to accept whoever you are . . . Did you really think our love was so conditional or so shallow?"

Perhaps the truest and most difficult test of all of a mother's love is caring for a child with a serious illness or with physical or mental disabilities. It is not unheard of for a parent to ignore or abandon a son or daughter who doesn't reflect what the larger world sees as "normal." Joseph Merrick, for instance, who came to be known as the Elephant Man because of the disease that radically distorted his facial features and enlarged his head, was kicked out on the street by an uncaring father and step-mother who couldn't stand the sight of him.

The 1985 film *Mask*, starring Cher and Eric Stoltz, told Rocky Dennis's true life story. Rocky's single mother Rusty never turned her back on her son; in fact, she did everything she could to assure that Rocky's life was filled with all the love and encouragement she could muster. Although her son suffered from a rare genetic defect known as craniodiaphyseal dysplasia that left his face severely deformed and eventually killed him at the age

of sixteen, Rusty insisted to everyone—hospital personnel, social workers, and school administrators—that Rocky be treated just as any "normal" child would be.

In one telling scene, the brash, tough-talking Rusty confronts a junior high school principal who, taken aback by Rocky's appearance, suggests it would be better if he enrolled in an institution where they could more aptly handle his "special needs." Rusty glares at him. "Do you teach algebra and biology and English here?" she asks. "Of course," the principal says. "*Those* are his needs," Rusty replies bluntly, before giving the man a profanity-laced dressing-down while Rocky looks on in amusement.

The bond that grew between mother and son during Rocky's short life was one of deep, abiding love and admiration for each other. Both, in a sense, were outcasts: Rocky because of his appearance, Rusty because of her raucous, hard-edged personality and her freewheeling biker lifestyle. But together they forged a life where self-pity was banished in favor of self-confidence, and the fear of death was replaced with an intoxicating love of life.

"She was the perfect mother for Rocky," says Rocky's half brother Joshua Mason. "A lot of mothers wouldn't have been so strong, would have coddled him, not given him a sense of himself. The movie . . . did capture that special thing between Rocky and Rusty."

And the scene that captured it best showed a sullen Rocky suffering from a case of nerves the morning before his first day at the new public school. Rusty encourages him to go, telling him that once the kids get to know him, they'll think he's terrific. "It takes time for people to get to like each other," she says. "I don't know why you think it should be any different with you."

"But I *am* different," Rocky reminds her.

"Yeah," Rusty says, "You're more beautiful on the inside than most people. Anybody who can't see that—"

"Screw 'em," Rocky adds, smiling, before taking a peck on the cheek from a glowing Rusty and heading out the door.

With Rusty's love, Rocky succeeded where the world expected him to fail. Doctors declared he would suffer acute mental retardation, but Rocky was a consistent honors student who even skipped a grade in school. They said he would gradually lose his sight; he told them, "I don't believe in being blind," and read until his final days. Although doctors had given him a death sentence by age seven, Rocky lived nine more years.

"People used to ask me if I felt cheated [having to raise Rocky]," says the real-life Rusty Dennis, who worked as a go-go dancer and door-to-door salesperson to help foot Rocky's medical bills. "I just told them that questioning it would drive you crazy. Why me? Well, why not me?"

Like countless other mothers, Rusty Dennis reminds us that unconditional love is not a conscious, pragmatic choice. It is simply the true language of a mother's heart.

Who is it that loves me and will love me forever with an affection which no chance, no misery, no crime of mine can do away? It's you, my mother.

—Thomas Carlyle

Chapter 4

A MOTHER'S
Protection

*It's after ten. I don't see why she has to have this pain . . . It's time
for her shot. Do you understand? Do something! All she has to do is hold on
until ten, and it's past ten. She's in pain. My daughter's in pain. Give her
the shot. Do you understand me? Give my daughter the shot!*

—Aurora Greenway, *Terms of Endearment*

In the animal kingdom there is nothing so fierce as a mother lion protecting her cubs. It's the same in the kingdom of humans—mothers can be absolutely ferocious when it comes to keeping their children from harm. While most mothers will never face a band of marauding hyenas, the civilized world is plagued with real dangers—gangs, sexual predators, and drunk drivers.

In 1910, author Rheta Childe Dorr wrote that a woman's place was in the home. But she added: "Home is not contained within the four walls of an individual home.

Home is the community. The city full of people is the family. The public school is the real nursery. And badly do the home and the family and the nursery need their mother."

The instinct to protect is so strong that mothers will often extend their protection to another mother's children. Author and historian Charlotte Gray observed, "Becoming a mother makes you the mother of all children. From now on each wounded, abandoned, frightened child is yours. You live in the suffering of mothers of every race and creed and weep with them. You long to comfort all who are desolate." That's how MADD, Mothers Against Drunk Driving, was formed.

In 1980, Candy Lightner's thirteen-year-old daughter, Cari, was killed by a drunk driver who had several prior offenses. In the aftermath of that tragedy, she discovered that the legal system wasn't doing enough to get repeat offenders off the road. Candy couldn't do anything to bring her own daughter back, but she could try to protect other children from the same fate.

Candy Lightner established MADD. In its first ten years, MADD successfully promoted the passage of more than 1,250 tougher state DUI laws, as well as a number of federal laws. Although Candy came to her crusade too late to save her own child, she has definitely saved scores of others.

Another example of mothers protecting others' children is the organization called the Million Mom March.

With MADD as its model, the Million Mom March came into existence to combat the gun violence that claims so many innocent children in this country. In August 1999, Donna Dees-Thomases, a New Jersey mother, was horrified when she read about a gunman who randomly shot at a group of children at a Jewish community center in Granada Hills, California. Even though her own children weren't involved, the news galvanized her. "The first five or ten women I spoke to about this, we all had the same reaction to what was going on in the country around guns," she said. "Our maternal instincts were just kicking in." A week later, she applied for a permit to march on Washington.

Nine months later, on Mother's Day of 2000, over

750,000 "mothers and others" gathered on the National Mall in Washington, D.C., to protest America's lack of effective gun laws. Another 150,000 to 200,000 marched in their own cities across the country. Since then, the Million Mom March has become a national, chapter-based organization and has joined forces with the Brady Campaign to Prevent Gun Violence. A mother's protective instincts moved nearly a million people to march.

To some mothers, there's no such thing as being "overprotective." But at some time, every mother has to fight the maternal instinct to shelter their children too much, because overprotected children are often ill-equipped to fend for themselves when out on their own. They become too dependent and don't develop the skill necessary to become fully functioning adults.

Oscar-winning actress Nicole Kidman, mother of two adopted children, was interviewed on *The Oprah Winfrey Show* about that very conundrum. Kidman is a parent who knows the anxiety of pitting motherly instinct against reason: "As a mother, your whole thing is to protect them, not want them to experience pain, not want them to go through things; but those, that adversity, a lot of times is the thing which gives you your character or your backbone. So that for me, is the struggle."

One of the best filmed illustrations of a mother's fierce protective nature is the five-Oscar winner from 1983, *Terms of Endearment,* which was adapted from famed Texas author Larry McMurtry's novel. A Pulitzer Prize winner for *Lonesome Dove,* McMurtry was also the creator of *The Last Picture Show.* Both novels were also made into movies. After spending a couple of years reading nineteenth-century novelists like Honoré de Balzac, Leo Tolstoy, and George Eliot, McMurtry was inspired to write *Terms of Endearment.* He says, "All three had taken a very searching look at the fibers and textures of life; I doubt I aspired to such profound achievement, but I did hope to search at least a little less superficially among the flea market of details which constitute human existence."

Terms of Endearment was a best-seller, and was originally optioned as a vehicle for Academy Award winner Jennifer Jones. That is, until writer-director James L. Brooks was brought onboard to direct the movie. At the time, Brooks was a veteran of television, responsible for huge successes like *The Mary Tyler Moore Show* and *Taxi,* but he'd never directed a feature. Nevertheless, his take on the project totally changed the casting—Jennifer Jones was out as Aurora Greenway—a character described as "a widow of a certain age, lively, imperious, demanding, unwilling to give up."

In Brooks's opinion, the right person to play Aurora was Shirley MacLaine because after Brooks auditioned a slew of actresses, "she was the only one who ever saw it as a comedy." They both knew that without a strong comedic balance, the movie, which ends tragically, could easily sink into syrupy sentimentality.

When Brooks wrote the screenplay, he kept McMurtry's distinctive Texas-tinged humor and his gifted insight into human interaction, and added a spicy "B story": Aurora's dalliance with ex-astronaut Garrett Breedlove (Jack Nicholson). Aurora and Garrett's sweet-and-sour fling is great entertainment and earned Nicholson an Oscar, but the heart and soul of the movie is the emotional tug of war between Aurora and her daughter, Emma (Debra Winger).

Aurora's intense love for her daughter is palpable,

and in the very first scene of the movie, we discover the depths of this fierce mother's protective nature. The scene is a flashback to Emma's first months of life. Emma is sleeping peacefully in her crib, and overly vigilant Aurora is convinced that her baby is dead because she isn't making any noise. She nearly climbs into the crib trying to make sure Emma is safe and is satisfied only when the baby wakes up and begins to cry. "That's better," says a relieved Aurora. The scene is funny and touching and desperate at the same time.

Aurora's protective nature extends to every aspect of Emma's life. The night before Emma's marriage to Flap Horton (Jeff Daniels) her "unsuitable" suitor, Aurora simply can't hold her tongue. Her frank dismissal of the couple's future together is a shock to Emma, but not a surprise.

"Emma, I'm totally convinced that if you marry Flap Horton tomorrow, it will be a mistake of such gigantic proportions, it'll ruin your life and make wretched your destiny," proclaims Aurora. Emma, wide-eyed, asks, "Why are you doing this to me?" Her mother replies bluntly, "You are not special enough to overcome a bad marriage." Since Aurora doesn't approve of the union, they agree she shouldn't attend the wedding, and indeed, Aurora doesn't.

In spite of the animosity between them, Aurora and Emma are still each other's best friends and biggest boosters. When Emma is diagnosed with terminal cancer, Aurora is devastated, but that doesn't mean she's any less protective of her child. One of the films most emotional and heart-wrenching moments is one director James Brooks mined from his own life. "This came from my sister," he says. "My sister was very seriously ill and there was pain connected to it and this came from that emotional experience."

In the scene, Aurora knows Emma is suffering, and it's a few minutes past the time the nurses were to have given her daughter her pain medication. When the nurses try to put her off, Aurora turns into a wild-eyed force of nature who will let nothing or no one delay her child's relief a moment longer.

"It's after ten," she announces to the nurses' station. "It's time for her shot. Do you understand? Do something!" Aurora demands, confronting one nurse and then another. "All she has to do is hold on until ten, and it's past ten." Aurora's anger and frustration builds. "She's in pain. My daughter's in pain. Give her the shot." Do you understand me? Give my daughter the *shot!*" Aurora screams. Then, when she finally gets her way, she instantly regains her composure and reverts to her normal well-mannered self, simply telling the nurses, "Thank you very much."

It's a powerful and unforgettable movie moment, a beautiful illustration of a mother's protective nature, and one of the scenes that helped earn Shirley MacLaine the

Best Actress Oscar that year. James Brooks, who won Oscars for Best Director, Best Picture, and Best Adapted Screenplay, says her performance was awe-inspiring, "I don't know how many people could [scream and yell] and know they were setting up that [thank you]."

MacLaine says she can relate to that protective aspect—her own mother was an aspiring actress who decided to stay home and raise Shirley and her younger brother, Warren Beatty, rather than subject them to the ups and downs of a show business life.

From the beginning of the species, it has been a mother's primary, hard-wired instinct to protect her children, no matter what the cost. What makes it so complicated and contrary to human nature is the knowledge that the best way to protect a child is to let that child experience life for itself. It means that being an effective mother is a difficult high-wire act, balancing instinct with reason to produce mothering that's not smothering.

God could not be everywhere and therefore he made mothers.

— JEWISH PROVERB

Chapter 5

A MOTHER'S

Sacrifice

Some people are going to think I'm crazy, but I don't care.
All that matters to me is Isaiah. . . . I'm doing this because I love him.
I really, really love him."

KHAILA RICHARDS, *Losing Isaiah*

Three days after a devastating earthquake in Iran killed 30,000 people, rescue workers digging through the rubble of a destroyed home found something astonishing. Buried beneath a mountain of brick and shattered concrete, and wrapped in the protective embrace of her dead mother, was a healthy, unscathed six-month-old girl.

Such instances of motherly courage and self-sacrifice never lose their power to inspire and amaze us. Whether we read about them in ancient myths or hear of them on the evening news, these heroic acts represent the epitome of selflessness and love, and we see in them something extraordinary. But for women engaged in the

dedicated, loving, and difficult work of raising children from day to day, the all-consuming instinct to shield them from harm, whatever the personal price, seems like the most natural thing in the world.

"Whether you talk to the mother of a newborn or the mother of a twenty-five-year-old, she will tell you how her stomach knots and worry descends whenever she senses that [her] child's well-being is at risk," says psychotherapist and author Janna Malamud.

And so they make sacrifices, both great and small. They willingly give up their time, their sleep, their careers, their dreams, and sometimes even their own lives, to give

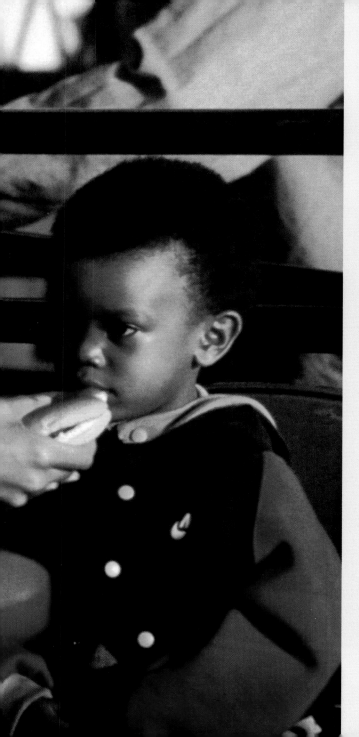

their children the best life they can. Take Margaret Bragg, mother of Pulitzer Prize–winning journalist Rick Bragg. Married to a violently abusive alcoholic who eventually abandoned the family, Margaret managed to raise three boys on her own, sweating in the Alabama cotton fields by day and taking in laundry and ironing by night. For nearly two decades she donned the same tattered dress—afraid even to attend church out of shame—while saving just enough to outfit her boys in new school clothes each year.

"[She] gave up her whole life for her children," says Bragg, whose 1997 best-selling autobiography, *All Over But the Shoutin'*, was a paean to the woman who did without so that he could raise himself above the poverty and ignorance of his surroundings. "By picking cotton, cleaning toilets for the gentry, doing worse, she made sure that her three surviving sons would not have to walk around ashamed, in ragged clothes."

"People are really heroic and have no idea that they are," said longtime advice columnist Ann Landers. "Women who are raising kids alone, holding down two jobs keeping things together—when I see what life is like for so many people, I've got to admire them. I don't know whether I could have survived some of the hardships and tragedies that I read about."

Some of these everyday heroes are mothers *and* grandmothers, like Geneva Dunbar. The fifty-one-year-old never expected to be raising children again at her age, having already watched her kids grow to adulthood, marry, and start families of their own. But when her daughter Lorisa was killed in the terrorist attacks of September 11, 2001, Geneva, like so many parents of victims of 9/11, left her own hopes and plans behind to care for her three motherless grandchildren.

Now she rises at dawn to prepare them for school and hits the pillow bone-weary after having cleaned, cooked, helped with homework, and tucked them in. And all the while, she suffers through the heavy grief of having lost her own child. "It's not what I planned," she says. "It is hard for me. But I'm so happy to be able to help in any way I can."

Author Rachel Billington has said that "true mothers must be made of steel to withstand the difficulties that are sure to beset their children." And sometimes the truest of mothers may not even be related to a child. "My mom, my angel, saved me," says Savanna Petricek about the woman who took her in when no one else would. "She adopted me, and both of us never looked back."

When Marilyn Petricek first laid eyes on the seven-year-old girl who was to become her daughter, she was stunned. Savanna had been severely abused and was burned on nearly 40 percent of her body. She could barely see, let alone read, and her teeth were badly infected. She slept in a burn suit, chronically wet the bed, and suffered from horrible nightmares.

"The first year-and-a-half, to be honest with you, was very difficult," recalls Marilyn, who never got a full night's sleep during that time. But after a half decade of love, nurturing, and tirelessly attending to Savanna's physical and emotional needs, Marilyn can look back on the sacrifices she made with joy and satisfaction. "I think the want and the will was always there, but no one would ever sit down with her and take the time to work with her," she says.

And for Savanna, now a well-adjusted teenager, the love of her adoptive mother has meant a new lease on life. "I just want people to know what it is to be loved by [Marilyn]," she says. "That's the best thing in the world, just to be loved."

Actress Jessica Lange, who has traveled the world publicizing the plight of orphans on behalf of UNICEF, and who helped arrange for the adoption of a Romanian child by an American family, understands intimately the sacrifices made by adoptive and foster parents. "My parents always impressed on us that it was important to help the needy," she says. "And I watched my grandmother raising other people's kids."

In 1995's *Losing Isaiah*, Lange had the chance to explore that relationship in depth as Margaret Lewin, a white social worker who adopts an African-American infant abandoned by his crack-addicted mother. When the mother, Khaila Richards (Halle Berry), resurfaces clean and sober three years later and is granted custody of the boy after an acrimonious court battle, the young Isaiah withdraws in depression, having lost the only family he knows, and the two women must set aside their resentments to do what is best for the child.

In the film's final scene, both women come to the tearful realization that while they each have made tremendous sacrifices on Isaiah's behalf—Margaret by raising the boy as her own and showering him with love, Khaila by kicking her poisonous habits and turning her life around to regain him and teach him of his African-American heritage—the desperate and confused three-year-old needs them both.

After receiving a frantic phone call from Khaila,

who despite her best efforts is unable to soothe the despondent Isaiah, Margaret agrees to meet. "I want you to go in there and hold him, tell him not to be scared anymore," Khaila begs her. "I'm not saying I'm giving him back to you. I'm just saying he's going to come live with you for a while until he understands all this. Some people are going to think I'm crazy, but I don't care. All that matters to me is Isaiah. . . . I'm doing this because I love him. I really, really love him."

"I love him, too," Margaret replies, embracing her former nemesis. And in their moment of reconciliation, these two women come to understand that the powerful bond between mother and child, a bond built on love and sacrifice, can't be shattered by courts or politics or racial division. In the end, they are *both* his mothers.

Like Lange, Berry's personal experiences found echoes in the film's controversial social issues. The daughter of an interracial couple, she was raised by a hard-working single mother who was white. "I couldn't imagine my mother being told she couldn't raise me because of the color of her skin," Berry says. "When you love a child, it doesn't matter what color your skin is."

The love of a mother is indeed blind to all obstacles, a selfless sacrifice that knows no bounds. "Oh, what a power is motherhood, possessing a potent spell," wrote the Greek playwright Euripides nearly twenty-five hundred years ago. "All women alike fight fiercely for a child."

A mother is a person who, seeing there are only four pieces of pie for five people, promptly announces she never did care for pie.

–TENNEVA JORDAN

Chapter 6

A MOTHER'S
Advice

Don't you think that everyone looks back on their childhood with a certain amount
of bitterness and regret about something? . . . Life marches on, Chels.
I suggest you get on with it.

—ETHEL THAYER, *On Golden Pond*

On August 18, 1920, a historic vote took place in Nashville, Tennessee. The state legislature, previously deadlocked over ratification of the Nineteenth Amendment, which would give American women the right to vote, had convened one last time to settle the matter. If the measure passed, women's suffrage would become the law of the land. With the vote tied, twenty-four-year-old lawmaker Harry Burn stepped up to cast the deciding ballot. Clutching a letter he had received the previous night from his mother urging him to vote in

43

favor of ratification, the young man declared, "I know that a mother's advice is always safest for a boy to follow," and gave women the victory.

Naturally, not every piece of advice from Mom has the capacity to change history. But even those less than earth-shattering motherly dictums like "remember to eat your vegetables" and "don't forget to look both ways before crossing the street," carry valuable weight, and given young Harry's predilection, we can be assured that in addition to a champion of women's rights, he was an extremely healthy and cautious individual.

"The best academy," wrote the poet James Russell Lowell, "[is] the mother's knee." But running that academy is no small chore. It's part and parcel of her job to prepare us for life's challenges, and from the time we're out of swaddling clothes, our mothers are called upon to act as our personal motivators, moral counselors, academic experts, romantic advisers, fashion consultants, and philosophical gurus—in short, our rudder on the ship of life. She's the one we can turn to in a pinch, the one who knows us like no one else, and the one who will tell us the truth when we need it—even if it's a hard lesson.

Take actress Halle Berry, the child of an interracial couple, whose white mother prepared her for a life of racial adversity by telling her early on that she would always have to work harder and be better than her peers to succeed. "[She told me] 'You can't take no for an answer—you're going to have to fight,'" Berry recalled after winning the 2002 Academy Award for Best Actress. "So it's normal for me, and I don't know how to act any other way. Now I'm inspired to try for things that I used to be too scared to try for in the past."

Of course, we don't always listen. At times, the instructive voice of our mother descends to a dull drone, and in our efforts to assert our own independence, we tune her out. Or we might not always grasp the importance of her words when we hear them; they fail to resonate until much later in life, after she is gone and our lives and circumstances have changed greatly. Then we hear them again, filtered through time and experience, and recognize the wisdom they possess.

"All those years of holding my hands over my ears, trying not to listen to the same old same old, were to no avail," admitted writer Felicity Stone, soon after her mother had passed away. "Her lectures, admonishments, and advice got through and are now an indelible part of my psyche, and part of my mother's legacy."

Like real life, art and literature abound with stories of mothers' advice heeded and ignored. Who can forget, for example, Katharine Hepburn's plainspoken homilies to her sullen middle-aged daughter in *On Golden Pond*?

As the adoring and eternally upbeat wife of curmudgeonly retired college professor Norman Thayer (Henry Fonda), Hepburn's Ethel seeks to forge a truce between

her husband and daughter, Chelsea (Jane Fonda), a grown woman on the verge of her second marriage who continues to harbor resentment against the cantankerous Norman for the slights he inflicted on her in childhood.

Ethel may be a fount of breezy enthusiasm, but her sanguinity is tempered by bluntness and hardheaded Yankee common sense. When Chelsea complains to her mother that although she'd like to have a friendship with her ailing dad, she can't seem to overcome the wounds of the past, Ethel responds sardonically, "Chels, Norman is eighty years old. He has heart palpitations and trouble remembering things. Just exactly when do you expect this friendship to begin?"

"This is Kate's real attitude in life," said the film's director, Mark Rydell. "You have a young daughter complaining of her agonies and blaming them on her past. What Kate does, in essence, is say, 'Pull yourself together, for God's sake. Get on with it.'"

And it is Ethel's directness with Chelsea that eventually leads to a reconciliation of sorts. In one of the film's most memorable mother-daughter scenes, Ethel finds Chelsea sulking over a dismissive comment made by Norman. "My father is a goddamn bastard," Chelsea snorts. "I've been answering to Norman my whole life. It makes me so mad, even when I'm three thousand miles away and I don't even see him!"

"Here we go again, your miserable childhood," Ethel replies. But while dishing out her tough talk, Ethel draws Chelsea close, stroking her head to let her daughter know that she understands her suffering. "Your father was overbearing, your mother ignored you, what else is new? Don't you think that everyone looks back on their childhood with a certain amount of bitterness and regret about something? It doesn't have to ruin your life, dar-

ling. You're a big girl now. Aren't you tired of it all? Life marches on, Chels. I suggest you get on with it."

On Ethel's advice, Chelsea sets aside her emotional baggage and offers Norman an olive branch, knowing that her father's stubbornness and age would never allow him to make the first move. By the film's end, the two have taken the first tentative steps toward patching up their relationship. "In the last act of life one doesn't change," Jane Fonda has said, echoing Hepburn's on-screen words of wisdom. "And one is wrong to expect it of a parent."

Like Chelsea Thayer Wayne, each one of us has those certain special words from our mother that will stay with us forever. We all gain a little piece of our mothers' souls—and more than a little bit of common sense—through their advice.

When a mother has done her work well, her insight and judgment remain a valuable resource to which her children can return again and again for solace and instruction. Her advice may make us uncomfortable, it may sometimes enrage us—but truth be told, she's usually right. And that includes washing behind your ears!

All I am I owe to my mother. I attribute all my success in life to the moral, intellectual, and physical education I received from her.

—GEORGE WASHINGTON

Chapter 7

A MOTHER'S
Trust

She will know I am waiting like a tiger in the trees,
ready to leap out and cut her spirit loose.

—YING YING ST. CLAIR, *The Joy Luck Club*

Two mothers had a terrifying experience on September 10, 2004, in East Brunswick, New Jersey. It was their child's first day of school—an already stressful day in a mother's life—and now they both feared that their sons were missing and might not be coming home.

Two boys were left unattended on two separate school buses. A six-year-old first grader got on the bus in the morning but did not get off at his scheduled stop in the afternoon. A three-year-old boy also did not get off his bus after his half-day preschool program. In each case, the driver found the boy hiding on their bus, drove them home, and placed them back into their mother's arms. Both mothers said they "had faith in God" and "trusted that my son knew how to get home."

Not all first days of school are as traumatic. Nonetheless, milestones in a son or daughter's life can be quite stressful on the bond of trust between mother and child.

Will they look both ways before crossing the street? Will she be safe on her first car date? Will he get hurt playing football? What kind of job will she have after graduation? Is he ever going to find the right girl? Are they really ready to be parents? These questions have plagued the minds of mothers year in and year out.

Christine Eghenian, an MFT and licensed psychotherapist in Hollywood, California, describes the strain of trusting offspring quite implicitly. "This child comes out of a mother completely dependent, and as they grow older it is the mother's job to do less and less and let their child do more and more. That's really hard because for years you are in complete control, and suddenly you have to let this being be their own person."

If a mother has done her job right, as far as instilling good values and proper judgment into her child, the relinquishing of control can make for some very profound rites of passage. This sense of freedom has been vividly captured in literature, particularly by one of America's most beloved authors, Dr. Seuss, in *Oh, the Places You'll Go*.

"You'll look up and down streets, Look 'em over with care," says the out-starting upstart of the book. "About some you will say, 'I don't choose to go there.' With your head full of brains, and your shoes full of feet, you're too smart to go down any not-so-good street."

Since the book was first published in 1990, millions of children have identified with this triumphant tome about life's great balancing act. Although loving protectors, mothers trust that they have instilled their children with enough confidence and wisdom to hopefully follow the right paths in life.

But choosing the right paths can become particularly intense. Amy Tan, whose best-seller *The Joy Luck Club* was culled from her experiences growing up in America with a very traditional Chinese mother, remembers that her mom's lack of trust was caused by her disapproval of Amy's choices as a teenager. This, in return, prompted Amy to turn her back on her Chinese heritage.

"I said to myself when I was seventeen, 'I'm not going to have anything to do with anything Chinese when I leave home—I'm going to be completely American,'" she says. "None of that Chinese torture or guilt ever again in my life. None of that responsibility crap, 'You owe it to your family. You have to do this for your family.' I was never going to speak to my mother again. She was disappointed in me? Well, I wasn't going to be around to disappoint her anymore."

The two eventually reconciled, as both mother and daughter came to understand and accept the views of the other, leading to a richer, more loving, and trusting relationship. "If you were to say to me when I was seventeen, 'You know, one day you're going to write a book about Chinese people and how much you love your mother,' I would have said, 'There is no way I would ever do that.' Those are the kinds of surprising changes that you can have in your life. Just be open to it."

Mothers the world over have cherished Wayne Wang's popular 1993 screen adaptation of Tan's novel that features scene after scene of the struggles Chinese mothers and daughters have in their maternal connections.

One particularly riveting exchange comes between Ying Ying St. Clair (France Nuyen) and her daughter Lena (Lauren Tom). Ying Ying is visiting Lena and her new husband in their home for the first time. Ying Ying sees a chart on the refrigerator supposedly dividing Lena and her husband's responsibilities and "love for each other equally." She also sees a frightening lack of trust and respect in Lena's spouse, similar to one of her own past relationships.

When Ying Ying was a youth in China, she was involved in an abusive relationship with a philanderer and killed their newborn son out of her hatred for her cruel husband. She remarried and had Lena, but she feels her spirit left with the spirit of her firstborn. Ying Ying

also feels she has passed this lack of strength and trust down to her daughter, leaving her vulnerable to her controlling spouse.

"My daughter will hear me calling, even though I have said no words," says Ying Ying. "She will feel in her heart the place where she hides her fears.

"What do you want from him?" Ying Ying prods her daughter when she enters the room. "Respect . . . tenderness," Lena answers, quivering. "Then tell him now," Ying Ying replies, empowering her. "Do not come back until he gives you those things, with both hands open."

"Children are inherently self-centered," notes psychotherapist Eghenian, "and will assume a responsibility for what happens to their mothers. When they grow up, they witness the kind of relationships their mother had with men and feel guilty they might have been responsible, and end up following the same path."

A mother's trust is very much like a revolving door, it's very cyclical. Just as trust can be lost, it can always be regained, and many factors can come into play to either speed up or slow down the pushing of that door. But once a child enters that revolving door at a trying time, the strength of trust in the maternal bond will always spin them back.

The mother-child relationship is paradoxical and, in a sense, tragic.
It requires the most intense love on the mother's side,
yet this very love must help the child grow away from the mother,
and to become fully independent.

—ERICH FROMM

Chapter 8

A MOTHER'S

Encouragement

Remework

Remember what I told you, Forrest, you're no different than anybody else.

—MAMA GUMP, *Forrest Gump*

A mother's encouragement is as vital to a growing child as sunshine is to a flower. Of the importance of encouragement, professor and author Leo Buscaglia, PhD, says, "Too often we underestimate the power of a touch, a smile, a kind word, a listening ear, an honest compliment, or the smallest act of caring, all of which have the potential to turn a life around." It can put children on the right path, inspire them, and give them the confidence to pursue their dreams, no matter how far-fetched or fantastic. Encouragement is a platform from which to launch a project, a career, a life.

Celebrated African-American writer and folklorist

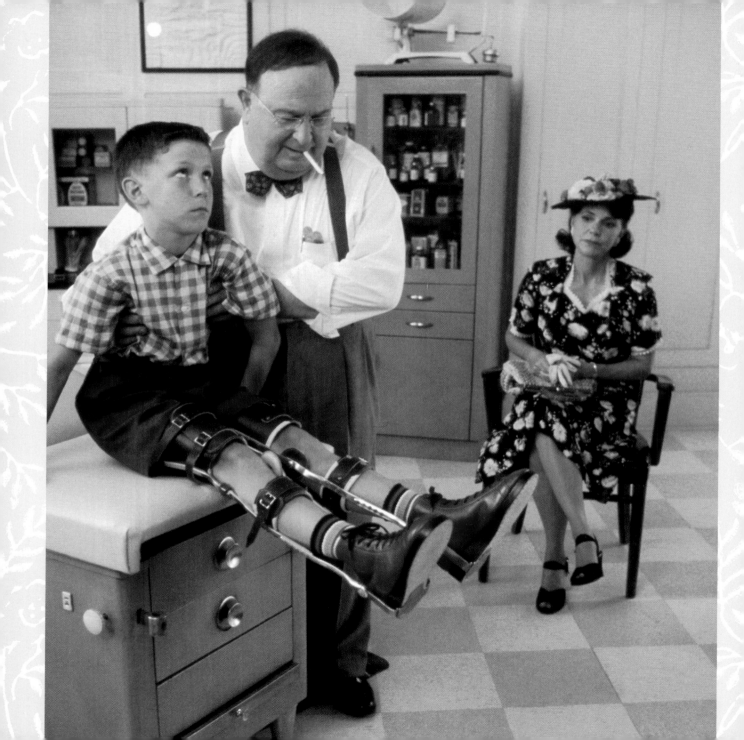

Zora Neale Hurston took her mother's advice and in 1937 had the courage to write *Their Eyes Were Watching God*, considered the first black feminist novel. Hurston is quoted as saying "Mama exhorted her children at every opportunity to 'jump at de sun.' We might not land on the sun, but at least we would get off the ground."

Writer George Matthew Adams observed, "There are high spots in all of our lives and most of them have come about through encouragement from someone else. I don't care how great, how famous or successful a man or woman may be, each hungers for applause."

Music and movie star Queen Latifah gives thanks to her mom for being her bedrock. During her sophomore year in high school Latifah (then known by her real name, Dana Owens) began rapping with two girlfriends in a group called Ladies Fresh. After her mother, Rita, told her she could be anything she wanted to be, she got serious about music. That encouragement led to Dana's recording and performing career, which has since branched into television, movies, and a production company of her own. The key was having her confidence built up by her mother. She even named herself "Queen" because she was "raised by a mother who told me every black woman is a queen."

Latifah says that kind of encouragement has a snowball effect. "Just me being my size and being on TV or being in a movie and succeeding is like, 'Hey, if she can do

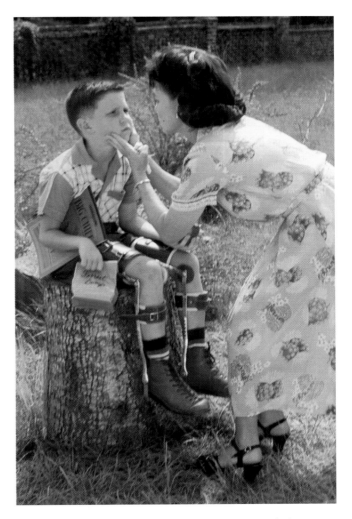

it, I can do it.' Sometimes you need that. I needed it growing up . . . luckily my mom gave me that encouragement."

South African born Oscar-winning actress Charlize Theron is another star who credits her mother's support and encouragement as a major reason for her success. Theron had huge obstacles to overcome to get to the top. First, she witnessed the death of her abusive alcoholic father, shot by her mother in self-defense during an attack.

That terrifying experience could have irreparably traumatized the fifteen-year-old. But her mother, Gerda, would have nothing of it, staying positive and keeping Charlize centered by encouraging her to pursue her dream of becoming a ballet dancer. Theron enrolled at the prestigious Joffrey Ballet School in New York City, but knee injuries ended her dreams of becoming a dancer. Once again her mother encouraged her, this time to try acting, and sent her a one-way airline ticket to Los Angeles.

This time, her mother's support paid off. Her acting career skyrocketed, capped off by her win of the 2004 Best Actress Oscar for her stunning portrayal of serial killer Aileen Wuornos in *Monster*. Gerda Theron was her daughter's date to the Academy Awards, and Charlize saved her most heartfelt thanks for the end of her acceptance speech. "Mom, you have sacrificed so much for me to be able to live here and make my dreams come true," Theron said, tearfully. "And there are no words to describe how much I love you."

From the Bible to the big screen, we see tales of mothers' encouragement and the life-altering effects of a mother's words.

The memorable movie *Forrest Gump* tells the story of a single mother who puts her heart and soul into making life as normal as possible for her slow-witted but good-hearted boy.

In the beginning of the movie, young Forrest is saddled with a subnormal IQ of seventy-five and a fearsome set of leg braces to correct the curvature in his spine. Determined not to allow her son to feel inferior, Mrs. Gump begins her crusade of encouragement, building up her son's self-esteem to prepare him for the taunting of the outside world. She sits him down on the front porch and tells him "Remember what I told you, Forrest, you're no different than anybody else. Did you hear what I said, Forrest, you're the same as everybody else. You are no different."

That encouragement follows Forrest throughout his adolescence and growth into manhood, serving as a moral compass as he finds himself thrust into situations—both personal and historical—beyond his control and understanding. Anchored by the self-assurance his mother has embedded in him, Forrest is able to weather each new trial in life, his unflappable innocence transforming everyone whose life he touches.

"Mama gave the support that Forrest feels all of his life," said Sally Field, who played Mrs. Gump. "[She was] the voice who gave him strength and wisdom and unconditional, full-out love."

Her most memorable piece of advice comes during the film's heartbreaking deathbed scene, as Forrest, responding to his dying mother's assertion that each person has his own destiny and must do the best with what God has given him, asks imploringly, "What's my destiny, Mama?"

"You're going to have to figure that out for yourself," she tells him. "Life is like a box of chocolates, Forrest. You never know what you're gonna get."

"Such a little bit of [Forrest's mother] goes such a long way, and you know that her words will be with him forever," said the film's producer Wendy Finerman.

Like the fictional Forrest Gump, children thrive on a mother's encouragement. Without it, even the most gifted person may let doubt trump talent. The impact of a mother's encouragement on her children cannot be overestimated. A few simple words can give someone the strength to take on the entire world.

Most of us, swimming against the tides of trouble the world knows nothing about, need only a bit of praise or encouragement—and we will make the goal.

—JEROME P. FLEISHMAN

Credits

Authored and produced by Joe Garner

Editorial/text assistance provided by Stuart Miller, Todd Schindler, Greg Reifsteck, and Bill Stroum

Narration written by Joe Garner

Footage and talent clearances managed by Suzy Vaughan Associates Inc. and Stephan Michaels

Original musical score composed and orchestrated by Richard Kosinski

Production coordinator, photo editor, and assistant to Joe Garner: Abigail Ray

DVD supervising editor: Chris Monte, Magic Hair Inc.

Audio production engineering by Mike Forslund

Main title, animation, and menu design by Castle Digital Design

Creative director: James Castle

Senior animator: Robert Dixon

DVD authoring provided by Los Angeles Duplication and Broadcast, Burbank, California

Motion picture clips provided by:

Forrest Gump, Terms of Endearment, Losing Isaiah courtesy of Paramount Pictures

The Joy Luck Club courtesy of Touchstone Pictures

Mask and *One True Thing* courtesy of Universal Pictures

My Big Fat Greek Wedding courtesy of Playtone and Gold Circle Films

On Golden Pond courtesy of Carlton Studios

We would like express our heartfelt gratitude to all of the wonderful actors who have graciously permitted the inclusion of their performances.

Photography Credits

All photos included in the *Life Is Like a Box of Chocolates . . . and Other Motherly Wisdom from the Movies* are listed by page number.

Big Wedding LLC images appear on the following pages: 4, 5, 6, 8.

Universal Studios Licensing LLLP images appear on the following pages: 13, 14, 15, 16, 20, 21, 22–23, 24.

Paramount Pictures/ Zade Rosenthal images appear on the following pages: 28, 32.

Paramount Pictures images appear on the following pages: 29, 31, 36, 37, 38–39, 40, 60.

Paramount Pictures/Phillip Caruso images appear on the following page: 58, 59.

Carlton Films images appear on the following pages: 45, 46, 47, 48.

© Buena Vista Pictures Distribution Inc. images appear on the following pages: 53, 54–55.